Yugioh Astrology

Yugioh Astrology

Astrological Guide to Decks, Duels, and More

Matthew Petchinsky

Apophis Enterprises LLC

Yu-Gi-Oh! Astrology: Astrological Guide to Decks, Duels, and More
By: Matthew Petchinsky

Message from Author

Hello, dear readers, I am a fan of Yu-Gi-Oh! I created this book because I felt inspired by my love of Yu-Gi-Oh! And Astrology. Please enjoy.

Disclaimer:

Disclaimer for "Yugioh Astrology: Astrological Guide to Decks, Duels, and More"

This book, "Yugioh Astrology: Astrological Guide to Decks, Duels, and More" ("the Guide"), is an unofficial, fan-made work and is not endorsed, sponsored, or affiliated with Konami Corporation, Kazuki Takahashi, or any of their subsidiaries or affiliates. The content within this Guide is created solely for entertainment purposes and should not be considered as an official guide to the Yu-Gi-Oh! Trading Card Game or any related products.

The Yu-Gi-Oh! name, trademarks, characters, card artwork, and all associated logos and designs are the exclusive property of Konami Corporation and Kazuki Takahashi. The use of such properties in this Guide is purely for creative expression and non-commercial fan-based activity. This Guide claims no ownership over any official trademarks or copyrighted materials mentioned herein.

The astrological interpretations and suggestions provided in this Guide are purely for entertainment and speculative thought. They are based on the author's personal interpretations and do not represent scientific knowledge or the views of the creators or licensors of the Yu-Gi-Oh! franchise.

Readers should be aware that the strategies, tips, and astrological associations discussed in this Guide are based on the author's personal views and experiences, and may not necessarily reflect optimal strategies or advice endorsed by professional Yu-Gi-Oh! players or the official rule guidelines set by the governing bodies of the Yu-Gi-Oh! Trading Card Game.

The information contained within this Guide is provided without warranty of any kind. The author and any contributors to this Guide will not be liable for any special, incidental, indirect, or consequential damages of any kind arising out of or in connection with the use or performance of information contained within.

This Guide may include links to other websites or content belonging to or originating from third parties. Such links are not an endorsement of those websites, nor the information contained therein, and the author and contributors disclaim all liability in regard to your access to and use of such sites.

Readers are encouraged to approach this Guide with a discerning mind and are reminded that it should not substitute for professional advice where that may be required.

The interpretations and recommendations contained herein are not meant to offend, defame, or misrepresent any people, groups, organizations, or entities. This book is not created with the intent to harm, slander, or malign any entity or individual involved directly or indirectly with the Yu-Gi-Oh! franchise.

By reading and using the Guide, you acknowledge that you understand this Disclaimer and agree to its terms. Should you disagree with any part of this Disclaimer, you are advised not to use or distribute this Guide.

Introduction to "Yugioh Astrology: Astrological Guide to Decks, Duels, and More"

Welcome to "Yugioh Astrology: Astrological Guide to Decks, Duels, and More", a unique blend of strategic gameplay and celestial wisdom. This guide is designed to introduce both novices and seasoned duelists to the intriguing synthesis of Yu-Gi-Oh! card duels and astrological insights, offering a new perspective on deck building and gameplay. Here, we explore the foundational elements of both Yu-Gi-Oh! and astrology, setting the stage for a deeper understanding of how these two seemingly distinct areas can interact harmoniously.

Overview of Yugioh

Yu-Gi-Oh!, originally conceived by Kazuki Takahashi in 1996 as a manga, has evolved into a globally celebrated trading card game (TCG). The essence of Yu-Gi-Oh! revolves around the "Duel Monsters" game, where players, known as duelists, use a collection of cards representing various monsters, spells, and traps to defeat their opponents. The strategic depth, immense variety of cards, and continuous evolution of the game rules have not only sustained its popularity over decades but have also made it a staple in competitive card gaming across the world.

The cultural impact of Yu-Gi-Oh! extends beyond just card duels. It has spawned an animated TV series, movies, merchandise, and even a dedicated fan base that creates its own formats and rules. Yu-Gi-Oh! is more than a game; it's a cultural phenomenon that encourages strategic thinking, creativity, and a shared community experience.

Basics of Astrology

Astrology is an ancient practice that interprets the influence of stars and planets on human affairs. Central to astrology are the Zodiac signs—twelve distinct segments of the sky each associated with its own set of traits and tendencies. These signs are often the first introduction many have to astrology, offering insights into personality, timing, and potential life events.

Beyond the signs, astrology also encompasses planets and houses, each adding layers of meaning. The planets, including the Sun and Moon, act as actors in the astrological drama, each with its distinct characteristics and themes. The houses, twelve divisions of the celestial sphere, represent different areas of life, from identity and resources to relationships and career. Understanding the interaction between signs, planets, and houses allows for a nuanced interpretation of an astrological chart.

Purpose of the Guide

This guide aims to fuse the strategic complexity of Yu-Gi-Oh! with the insightful world of astrology. Each Zodiac sign, planet, and house can offer unique insights into card choices, deck building, and duel strategies. For example, Mars, the planet of aggression and conflict, might inspire a more direct attack strategy, while Venus could suggest a deck focused on harmony and alliances.

Whether you're looking to personalize your deck to reflect your astrological strengths or seeking to understand the potential astrological tactics of your opponents, "Yugioh Astrology: Astrological Guide to Decks, Duels, and More" provides both practical advice and fascinating perspectives. By incorporating astrological elements into your dueling strategy, you can discover new dimensions of gameplay and perhaps even align your duels with the cosmos itself.

As we journey through the stars and across the dueling fields, let this guide be your compass, leading you to deeper insights and more rewarding duels. Let the celestial duel begin!

Chapter 1: Zodiac Signs and Deck Building

Welcome to the first chapter of "Yugioh Astrology: Astrological Guide to Decks, Duels, and More", where we delve into the synergy between Zodiac signs and Yu-Gi-Oh! deck building. Each Zodiac sign brings its own set of characteristics that can significantly influence how a duelist approaches deck construction, card choice, and overall strategy. Understanding these astrological aspects can give you a unique edge in your dueling tactics.

The Fire Signs: Aries, Leo, Sagittarius

Fire signs are known for their energetic, ambitious, and often aggressive traits. In Yu-Gi-Oh!, this translates into a playing style that is bold and direct, favoring quick victories and assertive moves.

- **Aries**: As the first sign of the Zodiac, Aries is associated with leadership and initiative. Duelists under this sign are likely to prefer fast-paced, aggressive decks that allow them to control the game from the outset. Cards that enable rapid, early attacks or strategies that can overwhelm opponents before they establish their defenses are ideal.

- **Leo**: Leo's commanding presence and desire to be in the spotlight translate well into decks that revolve around powerful, high-impact monsters. Leos thrive on dramatic plays and enjoy decks that allow them to exhibit their prowess through direct and devastating attacks.

- **Sagittarius**: Known for their love of adventure and exploration, Sagittarian duelists might incorporate elements of risk and variety into their strategies. This could mean a deck with unexpected combinations and a preference for dynamic, flexible tactics that can adjust to any play style.

The Earth Signs: Taurus, Virgo, Capricorn

Earth signs are all about practicality, reliability, and methodical approaches. In Yu-Gi-Oh!, this often leads to a preference for defensive and control-oriented decks that stand the test of time and strategy.

- **Taurus**: Taurus duelists gravitate towards stability and durability. They are likely to utilize decks that are resilient and capable of outlasting opponents through superior defense and resource management. Cards that ensure material advantage and fortify their field position are staples.
- **Virgo**: Virgos are meticulous and analytical, making them suited for complex control decks that require careful planning and execution. They excel with strategies that involve detailed knowledge of the game mechanics and interactions, often outmaneuvering opponents through precision and sustained control.
- **Capricorn**: Capricorn's disciplined nature fits well with strategies that build towards significant climactic moments. They might prefer decks that start slowly but grow over time, becoming nearly unstoppable. Capricorns appreciate structure and might opt for card combos that provide incremental advantages leading to a final, decisive victory.

The Air Signs: Gemini, Libra, Aquarius

Air signs are characterized by their intellectualism, communication skills, and adaptability, making them naturally inclined towards strategy-oriented and flexible decks.

- **Gemini**: Geminis are quick thinkers with a penchant for versatility, making them adept at using diverse and adaptive strategies. They may prefer decks that allow for rapid shifts in tactics depending on the flow of the game, utilizing cards that offer multiple options or paths to victory.

- **Libra**: Libra's focus on balance and fairness in all things can lead to a deck style that is well-rounded and strategic, aiming to counteract any moves made by the opponent. Libras might favor decks that specialize in negating or balancing the strengths of opponents, ensuring a fair play.
- **Aquarius**: Aquarians are innovative and forward-thinking, often choosing unconventional strategies that can catch opponents off guard. Their decks might include unexpected card choices or unique combos that reflect their originality and creative thinking.

The Water Signs: Cancer, Scorpio, Pisces

Water signs are deeply intuitive and emotionally intelligent, with a natural capacity for understanding underlying currents and dynamics.

- **Cancer**: Cancers are protective and intuitive, often building decks that adapt to their feelings about the opponent's tactics. They might use cards that protect their life points or that allow for reactive gameplay, ensuring they can respond to threats directly and personally.
- **Scorpio**: Scorpios are intense and strategic, with a knack for delving deep into the mysteries of the game. They may prefer decks that allow them to manipulate and control the duel through hidden threats or psychological tactics, often surprising their opponents with the depth of their strategy.
- **Pisces**: Pisces are adaptable and often empathetic, allowing them to intuitively understand their opponent's moves and strategies. They might favor decks that are versatile and fluid, capable of changing tactics mid-duel to match the shifting dynamics of the game.

By aligning your Zodiac traits with your deck-building strategies, you can enhance both your enjoyment and effectiveness in Yu-Gi-Oh! dueling. Let your sign guide you to decks that resonate with your personal strengths and watch how the stars can influence the outcome of your duels.

Chapter 2: Archetypal Cards and Their Astrological Correspondences

In "Yugioh Astrology: Astrological Guide to Decks, Duels, and More," we delve deeper into the mystique of the cosmos by aligning the iconic Tarot's Major Arcana with the strategic world of Yu-Gi-Oh! cards. This chapter explores the fascinating correspondence between these esoteric elements and the ruling planetary influences, offering duelists a profound way to harness celestial power through their decks.

Major Arcana for Each Sign

Each Zodiac sign can be associated with specific Tarot cards from the Major Arcana, reflecting the deep themes and characteristics inherent in each astrological symbol. These thematic connections can guide duelists in choosing Yu-Gi-Oh! cards that resonate with the same vibrational essence.

- **Aries (The Emperor)**: Reflecting leadership and authority, Yu-Gi-Oh! cards that command respect and dictate the pace of the game, such as "Fire King High Avatar Garunix," embody Aries' assertive spirit.
- **Taurus (The Hierophant)**: Embodying tradition and reliability, cards like "Grand Horn of Heaven" mirror Taurus's values, providing solid defense and stability in play.
- **Gemini (The Lovers)**: Symbolizing choices and intellect, Gemini resonates with cards like "Gemini Elf," which capture the duality and adaptability of this sign.
- **Cancer (The Chariot)**: Representing protection and sensitivity, "Mother Grizzly" mirrors Cancer's nurturing yet defensive nature.
- **Leo (Strength)**: Demonstrating courage and vitality, "Brotherhood of the Fire Fist - Lion Emperor" captures Leo's fiery, bold leadership.

- **Virgo (The Hermit)**: Reflecting introspection and analysis, "Pot of Duality" offers the strategic depth and careful planning synonymous with Virgo.
- **Libra (Justice)**: Symbolizing balance and fairness, "Balancer Lord" reflects Libra's core principles by equilibrating game dynamics.
- **Scorpio (Death)**: Representing transformation and control, "Plaguespreader Zombie" epitomizes Scorpio's profound ability to manipulate and rebirth.
- **Sagittarius (Temperance)**: Indicating optimism and adventure, "Soul of the Pure" reflects Sagittarius' quest for balance and exploration.
- **Capricorn (The Devil)**: Symbolizing ambition and persistence, "Grapha, Dragon Lord of Dark World" embodies Capricorn's relentless drive to dominate.
- **Aquarius (The Star)**: Representing hope and creativity, "Cosmic Blazar Dragon" aligns with Aquarius' visionary and innovative aspects.
- **Pisces (The Moon)**: Symbolizing intuition and mystery, "High Priestess of Prophecy" captures the deep, introspective nature of Pisces.

Planetary Influences

Each Zodiac sign is ruled by a planet whose characteristics can significantly influence the choice of Yu-Gi-Oh! cards and strategies. Integrating the planetary energies can enhance a duelist's alignment with their astrological strengths.

- **Mercury (Gemini, Virgo)**: As the planet of communication and intellect, Mercury's influence encourages strategies that involve quick thinking and adaptability. Cards like "Spellbook Magician of Prophecy" (for Virgo) and "Quickdraw Synchron" (for Gemini) embody Mercury's swift and versatile energy.

- **Venus (Taurus, Libra):** Governing love, beauty, and harmony, Venus inspires decks that focus on balance and interaction. For Taurus, "The Sanctuary in the Sky" provides a stable battleground; for Libra, "Elegant Egotist" ensures harmony and cooperation.

- **Mars (Aries, Scorpio):** The planet of war and aggression influences decks that are confrontational and controlling. Aries may use "Marauding Captain" for direct attacks, while Scorpio could opt for "Don Zaloog" to undermine opponents subtly.

- **Jupiter (Sagittarius, Pisces):** Symbolizing growth and wisdom, Jupiter's influence can lead to decks that support learning and expansion. Sagittarians might prefer "Sage of Silence," whereas Pisceans could choose "Salvage" to reclaim and reuse resources.

- **Saturn (Capricorn, Aquarius):** Representing discipline and karma, Saturn encourages strategies that are structured and revolutionary. Capricorns might lean towards "Timeater," and Aquarians towards "Alien Shocktrooper M-Frame" to disrupt conventional play.

- **Sun (Leo):** As a symbol of self and vitality, the Sun influences Leos to choose cards that are bold and dramatic, like "Solar Recharge."

- **Moon (Cancer):** Reflecting the subconscious and emotions, the Moon encourages Cancerians to opt for cards that protect and react, such as "Moon Mirror Shield."

By understanding these astrological and Tarot correspondences, duelists can construct decks that not only reflect their personal astrological alignments but also enable them to engage more deeply with the strategic and mystical aspects of Yu-Gi-Oh! gameplay. This synthesis of celestial and card-playing wisdom opens up a new realm of dueling dynamics, providing a richer and more rewarding dueling experience.

Chapter 3: Creatures and Corresponding Zodiac Signs

In the realm of "Yugioh Astrology: Astrological Guide to Decks, Duels, and More," the selection of creatures based on Zodiac signs can be a strategic and thematic choice that enhances a duelist's connection to their deck. This chapter explores the types of Yu-Gi-Oh! monsters that resonate with the elemental nature of each Zodiac group—Fire, Earth, Air, and Water—and how these creatures can be effectively utilized in gameplay.

Creatures for Fire Signs: Aries, Leo, Sagittarius

Fire signs are known for their passionate, energetic, and bold nature. Creatures such as dragons and warriors are perfect representations of these signs, embodying their fiery spirit and dynamic presence.

- **Dragons**: Dragons are a staple for fire sign decks due to their powerful, often destructive abilities that can quickly change the dynamics of the game. Cards like "Red-Eyes Black Dragon" (reflecting Aries' pioneering spirit), "Flame Swordsman" (mirroring Leo's theatrical and commanding presence), and "Blaster, Dragon Ruler of Infernos" (suiting Sagittarius' adventurous and risk-taking nature) can be particularly effective.

- **Warriors**: Warrior-type monsters often possess aggressive attributes and abilities to initiate quick and decisive actions, much like the fire signs themselves. "Marauding Captain" for Aries, "Heroic Champion - Excalibur" for Leo, and "D.D. Warrior Lady" for Sagittarius capture the assertive and courageous traits of these signs.

Creatures for Earth Signs: Taurus, Virgo, Capricorn

Earth signs value stability, practicality, and endurance. Golems and beast-warriors represent these qualities well, offering solid defense and reliable power in duels.

- **Golems**: Known for their formidable defense and substantial presence on the field, golems like "Gigantes" (for Taurus), which stabilizes through sheer strength, "Alpha The Electromagnet Warrior" (for Virgo), enhancing strategic field control, and "Block Dragon" (for Capricorn), providing resource durability, are quintessential for earth sign decks.
- **Beast-Warriors**: These creatures are renowned for their resilience and tactical strength. "Brotherhood of the Fire Fist - Buffalo" suits Taurus by enhancing resource accumulation, while "Zoodiac Ratpier" fits Virgo's meticulous nature, and "Gladiator Beast Laquari" reflects Capricorn's disciplined and strategic combat style.

Creatures for Air Signs: Gemini, Libra, Aquarius

Air signs are characterized by their intellectual, communicative, and flexible traits. Spellcasters and fairies are ideal for these signs, reflecting their mental agility and strategic finesse.

- **Spellcasters**: These creatures often have effects that manipulate the flow of the game, making them a perfect match for the intellectually inclined air signs. "Dark Magician" for Gemini offers versatile magic-based strategies, "High Priestess of Prophecy" for Libra ensures balance through knowledge, and "Aqua Madoor" for Aquarius symbolizes innovative magical tactics.
- **Fairies**: With their often complex and beneficial effects, fairies like "Neo-Parshath, the Sky Paladin" (for Gemini), facilitating swift and adaptable responses, "Archlord Kristya" (for Libra), enforcing fairness and order, and "Airknight Parshath" (for Aquarius), promoting revolutionary and high-impact plays, align well with the air signs' attributes.

Creatures for Water Signs: Cancer, Scorpio, Pisces

Water signs are intuitive, emotional, and often mysterious. Aqua and sea serpent monsters are natural choices for these signs, capturing their fluid and deep-seated emotional essence.

- **Aqua Monsters**: Known for their adaptability and often tricky abilities, aqua monsters like "Mother Grizzly" (for Cancer), which protects and reacts sensitively, "Abyss Soldier" (for Scorpio), adept at manipulating the field subtly, and "Mermail Abyssmegalo" (for Pisces), which provides flexible and powerful aquatic strategies, resonate with water signs.
- **Sea Serpents**: These creatures frequently embody the deep and enigmatic qualities of water signs. "Leviathan Dragon" suits Cancer's protective and nurturing tendencies, "Sea Dragon Lord Gishilnodon" reflects Scorpio's strategic depth, and "Poseidra, the Atlantean Dragon" captures Pisces' mystical and adaptable nature.

By selecting creatures that resonate astrologically, duelists can create decks that not only align with their personal astrological identity but also harness the inherent powers of these celestial influences. This approach offers a deeper, more intuitive connection to the game, enhancing both strategy and personal expression in duels.

Chapter 4: Lunar Phases and Duel Timing

In "Yugioh Astrology: Astrological Guide to Decks, Duels, and More," we explore how the lunar cycle can influence dueling strategy and timing. This chapter examines the various phases of the moon—New Moon, Full Moon, and the Waxing and Waning phases—and how each can be strategically leveraged to optimize gameplay, enhance deck performance, and align with astrological timings for tournaments and casual play.

New Moon: Initiating New Strategies

The New Moon represents new beginnings and is the ideal time to initiate new ventures. In Yu-Gi-Oh!, this is a powerful phase for experimenting with new decks and strategies.

- **Deck Testing and Tweaking**: During the New Moon, duelists are encouraged to test out new and untried decks. The energy of new beginnings supports taking risks and exploring creative or unconventional strategies that you haven't used before. This phase is perfect for tweaking and refining your approach based on initial feedback and impressions.
- **Setting Intentions**: Just as the New Moon is a time to set intentions for personal growth, duelists can set goals for their gameplay. Whether it's mastering a complex deck or integrating new cards effectively, use this time to focus your energies on upcoming challenges.

Full Moon: Harnessing Peak Energies

The Full Moon is a time of culmination and peak energy, making it ideal for capitalizing on the full potential of your deck.

- **Maximizing Deck Performance**: With the Full Moon illuminating possibilities, this phase is perfect for playing your best-tuned deck in competitive settings. The heightened energies can enhance your focus and intuition, allowing you to make the most of your strategic insights.
- **High Stakes Duels and Tournaments**: Plan to participate in tournaments or challenging duels during the Full Moon. The increased visibility and emotional intensity can boost your confidence and help you perform under pressure, utilizing the full strength of your deck.

Waxing Phases: Building Momentum

The Waxing Moon, growing fuller each night, symbolizes building momentum. It's an opportune time to develop your strategies and prepare for more significant challenges ahead.

- **Progressive Development**: As the moon waxes, consider this a phase for gradual improvement. Focus on strengthening your deck's weak points and enhancing your strengths. Incremental adjustments can be made to optimize every element of your deck.
- **Gathering Resources**: This is also a great time to acquire new cards that can enhance your deck. The building energy of the Waxing Moon supports expansion and growth, making it a favorable period for trading and obtaining cards that can provide a strategic edge.

Waning Phases: Reflecting and Recalibrating

As the moon wanes towards darkness, it symbolizes release and reflection, a period for duelists to reconsider and recalibrate their strategies.

- **Reflect on Past Duels**: Use the waning moon to analyze past performances and learn from defeats or challenges. What worked well? What didn't? This phase is about letting go of strategies that no longer serve you and preparing for the renewal that the New Moon will bring.

- **Pulling Back**: Reduce participation in high-stakes duels during this phase. Instead, focus on casual plays or practice matches that allow you to experiment without too much risk. It's a time for recovery and preparation, setting the stage for the next cycle of growth and competition.

Understanding and utilizing the phases of the moon can provide a significant strategic advantage in Yu-Gi-Oh! By aligning your dueling activities with these lunar cycles, you can maximize your effectiveness, adaptability, and intuitive connection with your deck, enhancing both your enjoyment and success in the game.

Chapter 5: Astrological Tactics for Duels

In "Yugioh Astrology: Astrological Guide to Decks, Duels, and More," understanding the intricate dance between your astrological profile and your dueling strategy can give you a unique edge in competition. This chapter delves into how your Sun sign, Moon sign, and Ascending sign can inform and guide your tactical approach in Yu-Gi-Oh! duels, helping you to harness your innate strengths and navigate your weaknesses.

Sun Sign Strategies: Tailoring Your Approach

The Sun sign in astrology represents your core identity, the essence of who you are. In Yu-Gi-Oh!, leveraging the traits of your Sun sign can help you to develop a dueling style that resonates with your inherent nature.

- **Fire Signs (Aries, Leo, Sagittarius):** Duelists under these signs should adopt aggressive and dynamic strategies, taking the initiative and maintaining offensive pressure to overwhelm opponents quickly.

- **Earth Signs (Taurus, Virgo, Capricorn):** If your Sun sign falls under Earth, your dueling approach should be more defensive and strategic, focusing on building a strong, unyielding position while patiently waiting for the optimal moment to strike.

- **Air Signs (Gemini, Libra, Aquarius):** Air sign duelists excel in adaptable and intellectual strategies. Employing varied tactics and maintaining flexibility will allow you to outthink and outmaneuver your opponents.

- **Water Signs (Cancer, Scorpio, Pisces):** For Water signs, intuition and emotional intelligence guide your play. Utilize decks that adapt to changing circumstances and focus on reading your opponent's strategies and emotions to gain an advantage.

Moon Sign Intuitions: Leveraging Subconscious Impulses

Your Moon sign governs your emotions and your subconscious, influencing how you react under stress or decision-making in uncertain situations.

- **Understanding Your Inner Impulses**: By recognizing the traits of your Moon sign, you can better understand your instinctual reactions during duels. For instance, a Moon in Scorpio might subconsciously strategize to control and manipulate the game, whereas a Moon in Pisces might intuitively understand the flow of play.
- **Enhancing Decision-Making**: Use your Moon sign to fine-tune your decision-making process. For example, if your Moon is in a Cardinal sign, you might be naturally inclined to take the lead in making swift decisions. If it's in a Mutable sign, you might excel in adapting your strategy mid-duel.

Ascending Sign Dynamics: Crafting Your Dueling Persona

The Ascendant or Rising sign shapes your outer self, the persona you project to the world, and how others perceive you.

- **Guiding Public Persona**: This can be particularly important in a public setting like tournaments, where first impressions can influence the psychological aspect of duels. An Ascendant in Leo might project confidence and dominance, potentially intimidating opponents.
- **Tactical Implications**: Your Ascendant can help determine the most effective way to present your strategies to others. For example, a Sagittarius Ascendant might do well with a straightforward, honest approach, while a Virgo Ascendant could find success in meticulous and detailed planning visible to others, showcasing their thoroughness.

Incorporating these astrological elements into your Yu-Gi-Oh! tactics not only personalizes your dueling experience but also enhances your natural abilities and compensates for potential weaknesses. By aligning your strategies with your astrological signs, you create a powerful synergy that can be both fulfilling and effective in competitive play. As you integrate these insights, observe how your duels evolve and how opponents respond to your astrologically informed approach, refining your tactics as you grow in both astrological wisdom and dueling prowess.

Chapter 6: Zodiac Sign Synergies and Rivalries

In "Yugioh Astrology: Astrological Guide to Decks, Duels, and More," understanding the interplay between different Zodiac signs can significantly impact your strategy in both cooperative and competitive settings. This chapter delves into the dynamics of astrological compatibility and rivalry, offering insights into how these relationships can influence tag team duels, joint deck building, and strategies for handling challenging opponents.

Compatible Signs: Enhancing Teamwork and Cooperation

Astrological compatibility can offer a strategic advantage in tag team duels and collaborative deck building, enhancing the synergy between players.

- **Fire and Air Compatibility**: Fire signs (Aries, Leo, Sagittarius) naturally synergize with Air signs (Gemini, Libra, Aquarius). Fire's dynamic and aggressive energy pairs well with Air's intellectual and strategic approach. This combination can lead to explosive offensive strategies combined with clever tactical planning.
- **Earth and Water Compatibility**: Earth signs (Taurus, Virgo, Capricorn) find harmony with Water signs (Cancer, Scorpio, Pisces). The practical and stable nature of Earth provides a solid foundation for Water's intuitive and adaptive tactics, creating a balanced team that can both defend strongly and respond fluidly to changing duel scenarios.
- **Using Compatibility in Duels**: In tag team duels, compatible sign pairs should plan their decks to complement each other's strengths. For instance, a Leo could focus on high-impact monsters while their Libra partner manages control and balance, ensuring their strategies effectively mesh to control the field and overwhelm opponents.

Competitive Signs: Navigating Rivalries and Opposition
Understanding the natural tension between certain Zodiac signs can help you prepare for duels with astrologically challenging opponents, turning potential weaknesses into strengths.

- **Fire vs. Water Rivalries**: Fire signs often clash with Water signs due to their opposing natures. Fire's aggressiveness can be tempered by Water's ability to adapt and absorb pressure. When facing Water sign opponents, Fire sign duelists should consider incorporating elements that disrupt emotional play and force quick decisions, countering Water's natural fluidity.
- **Earth vs. Air Rivalries**: Earth signs' methodical approach can sometimes be disrupted by Air signs' flexibility and unpredictability. In these matchups, Earth sign players should focus on fortifying their defenses and gradually undermining Air's strategies through consistent pressure and stability.
- **Strategic Approaches to Rivalries**: Understand the elemental weaknesses of your sign and plan countermeasures. For example, an Aries duelist facing a Pisces might use cards that restrict spell and trap activation to limit Pisces' strategic options, while a Capricorn might use disruption tactics like "Effect Veiler" or "Ghost Ogre & Snow Rabbit" to neutralize Gemini's quick-play strategies.

Utilizing Synergies and Anticipating Rivalries in Deck Building
When building decks, consider your Zodiac sign's characteristics and how they can be amplified or balanced by the signs of potential teammates or opponents:

- **Synergistic Deck Building**: For teammates, integrate card choices that enhance each other's playing style. A Sagittarius and an Aquarius could build a deck that focuses on big, game-changing plays while maintaining flexibility and surprise elements.

- **Rivalry-Based Deck Preparation**: When preparing for a duel against a competitive sign, tailor your deck to exploit their weaknesses. For example, Scorpio duelists might add more cards that control or manipulate the opponent's hand and graveyard when preparing to face a Taurus, potentially destabilizing Taurus's reliance on resource control.

Understanding and applying the principles of Zodiac sign synergies and rivalries can transform how you approach Yu-Gi-Oh! duels, offering deeper strategic layers and more meaningful interactions on the dueling field. This astrological approach encourages players to think creatively and strategically, enhancing both the competitiveness and enjoyment of the game.

Chapter 7: Best Cards for Each Zodiac Sign

In "Yugioh Astrology: Astrological Guide to Decks, Duels, and More," selecting cards that resonate with the distinctive characteristics of each Zodiac sign can significantly enhance a duelist's personal style and effectiveness. This chapter provides detailed recommendations of specific Yu-Gi-Oh! cards that align well with the inherent qualities of each sign from Aries to Pisces, helping to maximize strategic advantages and personal connection to the game.

Aries (March 21 - April 19)

Traits: Energetic, aggressive, pioneering

Recommended Cards:

- **Fire Formation - Tenki**: Enhances the searching capabilities, fueling Aries' need to lead and attack swiftly.
- **Ultimate Conductor Tyranno**: A powerful monster that can be summoned quickly and disrupts the opponent's field, embodying Aries' aggressive and dominating nature.

Taurus (April 20 - May 20)

Traits: Reliable, patient, resource-oriented

Recommended Cards:

- **The Monarchs Erupt**: This card represents Taurus' love for control and stability, negating the effects of all other monsters on the field.
- **Marshmallon**: Symbolizes Taurus' defensive and enduring nature, providing protection and resilience in battle.

Gemini (May 21 - June 20)

Traits: Adaptable, communicative, intelligent

Recommended Cards:

- **Gemini Elf**: Reflects Gemini's dual nature and intellectualism.
- **Magical Mallet**: Offers versatility and decision-making opportunities, matching Gemini's adaptable gameplay.

Cancer (June 21 - July 22)

Traits: Protective, emotional, intuitive
Recommended Cards:

- **Mother Grizzly**: This card's protective nature and ability to replace itself with another water monster echoes Cancer's nurturing tendencies.
- **Moon Mirror Shield**: Represents Cancer's ability to adapt and protect, ensuring the equipped monster can always outbattle opponents.

Leo (July 23 - August 22)

Traits: Bold, dramatic, leader
Recommended Cards:

- **Fire King High Avatar Garunix**: Represents Leo's fiery and regenerative qualities, as it can rise from the ashes after being destroyed.
- **Brotherhood of the Fire Fist - Lion Emperor**: Embodies Leo's leadership and flair for dramatic gameplay.

Virgo (August 23 - September 22)

Traits: Analytical, meticulous, practical
Recommended Cards:

- **Pot of Duality**: Allows for careful planning and strategic execution, resonating with Virgo's methodical approach.

- **Traptrix Rafflesia**: This card represents Virgo's detail-oriented and controlled style, setting traps and managing the field meticulously.

Libra (September 23 - October 22)
Traits: Balanced, fair, diplomatic
Recommended Cards:

- **Balance of Judgment**: Offers a chance to even the playing field, aligning with Libra's innate desire for fairness.
- **Dark Bribe**: Demonstrates Libra's diplomatic approach, providing negotiation through card interactions.

Scorpio (October 23 - November 21)
Traits: Intense, resourceful, strategic
Recommended Cards:

- **Plaguespreader Zombie**: Allows for tactical graveyard manipulation, fitting Scorpio's strategic depth.
- **Goyo Guardian**: Embodies Scorpio's intense and controlling nature, capturing opponents' monsters for personal use.

Sagittarius (November 22 - December 21)
Traits: Optimistic, adventurous, philosophical
Recommended Cards:

- **Soul of the Pure**: Matches Sagittarius' optimistic and adventurous spirit by increasing Life Points.
- **Foolish Burial**: Reflects Sagittarius' philosophical approach to risk and benefit, sending cards from the deck to the graveyard for strategic setups.

Capricorn (December 22 - January 19)
Traits: Disciplined, managing, ambitious
Recommended Cards:

- **Card of Demise**: Draws power through discipline, as it requires the duelist to use up their hand; perfect for the methodical Capricorn.
- **Timeater**: Reflects Capricorn's controlled and time-managing skills, manipulating the pace of the duel.

Aquarius (January 20 - February 18)
Traits: Innovative, humanitarian, independent
Recommended Cards:

- **Cosmic Fortress Gol'gar**: Symbolizes Aquarius' ability to innovate and recycle resources effectively.
- **Alien Shocktrooper M-Frame**: Demonstrates Aquarius' affinity for technology and unique gameplay.

Pisces (February 19 - March 20)
Traits: Compassionate, adaptable, intuitive
Recommended Cards:

- **High Priestess of Prophecy**: Uses intuition to reveal and manipulate the deck, mirroring Pisces' mystical and foresightful qualities.
- **Salvage**: Represents Pisces' ability to recover and adapt, retrieving resources from the graveyard.

These card selections not only enhance the playing style suited to each Zodiac sign but also allow duelists to engage more deeply with their decks, creating a more personalized and astrologically aligned dueling experience.

Chapter 8: Celestial Events and Their Impact on Duels

In "Yugioh Astrology: Astrological Guide to Decks, Duels, and More," we explore how celestial events can influence dueling strategies and outcomes. This chapter delves into how significant astrological events such as eclipses, equinoxes, solstices, and planetary transits can be strategically utilized to enhance gameplay and optimize the timing of major duels or tournaments.

Eclipses, Equinoxes, and Solstices

These astronomical events are not only significant markers in the cycle of the year but also offer unique opportunities for setting the stage for major duels and tournaments.

- **Eclipses**: Solar and lunar eclipses are powerful events for setting transformative goals or initiating major shifts in strategy. Eclipses can serve as a dramatic backdrop for high-stakes duels where players may want to unveil a new deck or a surprise strategy. Planning a tournament around an eclipse can heighten the emotional and psychological intensity, making for a memorable and impactful event.

- **Equinoxes (Spring and Autumn)**: Equinoxes, when day and night are of equal length, symbolize balance and harmony. They are ideal times for tournaments that promote a level playing field where strategic thinking and calm decision-making prevail over brute force. Use this time to focus on decks that require a balanced approach to offense and defense.

- **Solstices (Summer and Winter)**: The solstices mark the peaks of solar power and withdrawal. The Summer Solstice, with its emphasis on abundance and energy, is perfect for aggressive, fast-paced dueling styles. In contrast, the Winter Solstice, a time of reflection and conservation, might favor strategies that focus on defense and resource management.

Planetary Transits

The movement of planets through different Zodiac signs and houses can significantly affect dueling style, influencing the energy and dynamics of gameplay.

- **Mars Transits**: When Mars transits a sign, it energizes the themes of aggression and competition associated with that sign. If Mars enters Aries, for example, duelists might find that aggressive, fast-paced strategies are more effective. During such transits, consider enhancing your deck with cards that favor quick, decisive actions and confrontational tactics.

- **Mercury Transits**: Mercury governs communication and intellect. Its transit through different signs can affect strategic thinking and negotiation during a duel. When Mercury is in Gemini, the focus might shift to quick thinking and adaptability. Duelists should consider using decks that benefit from a high degree of strategic planning and real-time decision-making.

- **Venus Transits**: Venus influences harmony and the relationships between players. When Venus transits a sign like Libra, the focus can shift towards fairness and equilibrium in gameplay. This might be a good time for tag-team duels where cooperation between partners is highlighted. Decks that allow for mutual benefits and shared strategies could be particularly effective.

- **Jupiter Transits**: Known for bringing expansion and luck, Jupiter's transit through any sign can amplify the qualities of that sign in the context of dueling. For example, if Jupiter transits Sagittarius, duelists might find that luck and a positive attitude can dramatically influence the outcome of their matches. Incorporating cards that rely on chance or that provide significant boosts under certain conditions can be a wise strategy.

By aligning dueling activities with these celestial events and planetary influences, duelists can leverage the inherent energies of the cosmos to enhance their strategic approach and performance in Yu-Gi-Oh! duels. Whether planning a tournament, testing a new deck, or engaging in a high-stakes duel, understanding the impact of these astrological factors can provide a competitive edge and a deeper connection to the universal forces that influence our lives.

Chapter 9: Advanced Astrological Techniques for Yu-Gi-Oh!

In "Yugioh Astrology: Astrological Guide to Decks, Duels, and More," we delve into advanced astrological techniques that provide duelists with a deeper understanding of how celestial influences can be utilized to enhance personal dueling styles and strategic timing. This chapter explores the application of birth charts for deck customization and techniques for electing astrologically favorable times to maximize success in duels and tournaments.

Using Birth Charts to Customize Decks

A duelist's natal chart, or birth chart, is a snapshot of the celestial positions at the exact moment of their birth, offering insights into their personality, strengths, and challenges. Analyzing a birth chart can guide duelists in customizing their decks to reflect and enhance their inherent astrological traits.

- **Identifying Key Planetary Positions**: Start by identifying the Sun, Moon, and Ascendant (Rising Sign) positions in the birth chart, as these are primary indicators of a person's character. For instance, a Sun in Aries might suggest a preference for aggressive and fast-paced decks, while a Moon in Pisces could indicate a strategy that benefits from adaptability and intuitive play.
- **Elemental Balance**: Assess the balance of elements (Fire, Earth, Air, Water) in the chart. A dominance of Fire might call for a dynamic and action-oriented deck, whereas a predominance of Water suggests a deck that can capitalize on emotional intelligence and fluid tactics.
- **Planetary Aspects**: Look at the aspects (angles) between planets, which can reveal dynamic interactions within the personality. For example, a Mars-Pluto conjunction might indicate a duelist who thrives on intense and transformative strategies, perhaps suggesting a deck that focuses on significant card transformations and combo plays.

- **Ruling Planets and Houses**: Consider the ruling planet of the Ascendant and its placement. A duelist with Mars as a ruling planet, positioned in the strategic tenth house, might excel with a deck that enables them to assert control and dominance in competitive scenarios.

Electing Astrologically Favorable Times

Electing the most auspicious times for starting duels or entering tournaments involves analyzing planetary positions and movements to select moments that align favorably with a duelist's personal astrological configurations.

- **Moon Phases and Aspects**: Begin with the Moon, as its phase and aspects it forms with other planets are crucial for timing in astrology. Initiating something new, like starting a tournament, is generally best done when the Moon is waxing (growing fuller), which symbolizes growth and buildup.
- **Planetary Hours**: Each hour of the day is ruled by a different planet, based on an ancient system of timekeeping. Electing a time when a beneficial planet (like Jupiter for luck and success, or Venus for harmony and popularity) rules the hour can enhance the likelihood of success.
- **Void of Course Moon**: Avoid starting important matches during the Moon's Void of Course period (after making its last major aspect before changing signs). Actions begun during this time often do not come to fruition or have unexpected outcomes.
- **Transits to Natal Planets**: Consider transits, which are current planetary movements that activate points in the personal birth chart. Choosing a time when beneficial transits occur to key natal planets can provide a competitive edge. For example, Jupiter transiting natal Mercury might be an excellent time for strategic thinking and communication.

By employing these advanced astrological techniques, duelists can create decks that truly reflect their personal cosmic signature and select times that align with celestial patterns to maximize their potential for success. This sophisticated approach allows players to engage with Yu-Gi-Oh! on a deeper level, integrating universal energies with the earthly tactics of the game.

Chapter 10: Continuing Your Astrological and Yu-Gi-Oh! Journey

In "Yugioh Astrology: Astrological Guide to Decks, Duels, and More," the journey through the realms of astrology and Yu-Gi-Oh! is just beginning. This chapter provides resources and practices to further deepen your understanding and enhance your skills in both fields. As you continue to explore the synergistic relationship between celestial influences and card dueling strategies, these guidelines will support your growth and development as a well-rounded duelist and astrologer.

Resources for Further Study

Expanding your knowledge in both Yu-Gi-Oh! and astrology can lead to more refined and successful dueling strategies, as well as a richer personal and spiritual life. Here are some recommended resources to continue your exploration:

- **Books:**
  - **Yu-Gi-Oh!:**
    - "Yu-Gi-Oh! Official Handbook" by Tracey West provides an excellent introduction and comprehensive details about the game.
    - "Yu-Gi-Oh! Duelist's Resource: Strategies and Tips" by Eliot Carter offers advanced tactics and deck-building advice.
  - **Astrology:**
    - "The Only Astrology Book You'll Ever Need" by Joanna Martine Woolfolk is a comprehensive guide to astrology for beginners and experienced practitioners alike.

- ■ "Parker's Astrology: The Definitive Guide to Using Astrology in Every Aspect of Your Life" by Julia and Derek Parker provides in-depth insights and practical applications of astrological principles.
- **Online Resources:**
  - ◦ **Yu-Gi-Oh!:**
    - ■ Dueling Network or YGOPro are platforms to practice your dueling skills against duelists from around the world.
    - ■ The official Konami site and forums for staying updated on rule changes, new card releases, and tournament dates.
  - ◦ **Astrology:**
    - ■ Astro.com offers free chart calculations and in-depth interpretations.
    - ■ Café Astrology provides a wealth of articles, tutorials, and personalized reports that make astrology accessible and practical.
- **Communities:**
  - ◦ Join online forums and social media groups such as Reddit's r/yugioh and r/astrology where enthusiasts discuss strategies, experiences, and advice.
  - ◦ Local clubs or meetups for both Yu-Gi-Oh! and astrology can be found through platforms like Meetup.com, offering opportunities to connect with like-minded individuals.

Developing Your Intuitive Connection

Deepening the intuitive link between your astrological insights and Yu-Gi-Oh! strategies involves both practical exercises and reflective practices:

- **Daily Card Draws:** Start each day by drawing a single Yu-Gi-Oh! card and a tarot card. Reflect on how the day's astrological aspects might influence the attributes of these cards and how this could translate into your dueling strategies or life decisions.

- **Meditative Practices**: Spend time meditating on your deck and your astrological chart. This can help to foster a deeper connection between your subconscious intuition and the strategic choices you make during duels.

- **Journaling**: Keep a journal of your duels and astrological observations. Note the moon phase, planetary alignments, and the outcome of your duels. Over time, patterns may emerge that can offer insights into optimal times for different kinds of dueling strategies.

- **Astrological Tracking**: Begin tracking the transits that occur during your most successful and challenging duels. This can help to identify which planetary movements seem to influence your gameplay positively or negatively.

As you continue to integrate these astrological and intuitive practices with your Yu-Gi-Oh! strategies, you will likely discover an increasingly profound synergy between your inner wisdom and your external gameplay. This journey is one of personal growth, strategic enhancement, and most importantly, enjoyment of both the ancient art of astrology and the modern challenge of Yu-Gi-Oh! dueling.

Appendix A: Glossary of Yu-Gi-Oh! and Astrological Terms
This appendix serves as a comprehensive guide to the key terms used throughout "Yugioh Astrology: Astrological Guide to Decks, Duels, and More." Familiarizing yourself with these terms will enhance your understanding of both the game of Yu-Gi-Oh! and the study of astrology, aiding in the application of advanced strategies and concepts discussed in the guide.

<u>**Yu-Gi-Oh! Terminology**</u>
Basic Terms

- **Deck**: The collection of cards each player uses during a duel. A typical competitive deck contains 40 to 60 cards, which include a combination of Monster, Spell, and Trap cards.
- **Duel**: The contest between two players, each using their deck to strategically reduce the opponent's Life Points to zero, or meet another win condition such as certain card effects.

Card Types

- **Monster Cards**: The primary type of cards used in the game. Players summon monsters to the field to attack their opponent or defend against attacks. Monster cards include:
  - **Normal Monsters**: Simple monsters with no effects.
  - **Effect Monsters**: Monsters that have special abilities which can be activated under certain conditions.
  - **Ritual Monsters**: Monsters that can only be summoned through specific Ritual Spell Cards.
  - **Fusion Monsters**: Monsters created by fusing two or more specific monsters, usually with the help of a spell or other card effect.

- **Synchro Monsters**: Monsters that require a Tuner monster and one or more non-Tuner monsters to be summoned.
- **Xyz Monsters**: Summoned by stacking two or more monsters of the same level and using them as Xyz Materials.
- **Pendulum Monsters**: Monsters that can be played as either monsters or Spell Cards and can allow a player to perform multiple summons at once.
- **Link Monsters**: Monsters with no level that are summoned by sending materials to the graveyard based on their Link Rating.
- **Spell Cards**: Provide various effects that can alter the course of the game. They are divided into several categories:
  - **Normal Spells**: Once activated, their effect occurs and then the card is sent to the Graveyard.
  - **Continuous Spells**: Remain on the field and provide ongoing effects.
  - **Equip Spells**: Attached to a specific monster and alter its abilities or stats.
  - **Field Spells**: Affect the entire field, providing benefits or detriments to one or both players.
  - **Quick-Play Spells**: Can be activated during any phase of yours or your opponent's turn.
  - **Ritual Spells**: Used to Ritual Summon Ritual Monsters.
- **Trap Cards**: Designed to surprise the opponent by being set facedown and activated in response to certain actions. Categories include:
  - **Normal Traps**: Activate in response to actions and are then sent to the Graveyard.
  - **Continuous Traps**: Stay on the field and have ongoing effects.
  - **Counter Traps**: Fast-acting traps that can negate and respond to other cards' activations.

Gameplay Mechanics

- **Life Points**: Each player starts with a predetermined amount of life points (usually 8,000). The primary objective is to reduce the opponent's Life Points to zero.
- **Field**: The game board where cards are played. Includes specific zones for Monster Cards, Spell and Trap Cards, the Deck, Graveyard, and in some formats, Extra Deck zones.
- **Phase**: A turn is divided into several phases, which include the Draw Phase, Standby Phase, Main Phase 1, Battle Phase, Main Phase 2 (optional), and End Phase.
- **Synchro Summon, Xyz Summon, Pendulum Summon, Link Summon**: Special methods of summoning that utilize different rules and card interactions to bring more powerful monsters to the field.

Advanced Concepts

- **Chain**: A sequence of card effects that resolve in reverse order of their activation. Understanding how to create and resolve chains is key to mastering more complex interactions and timings in the game.
- **Banlist (Forbidden, Limited, and Semi-Limited Lists)**: A regularly updated list that restricts certain powerful cards to ensure balanced gameplay. Cards can be forbidden (zero copies in the deck), limited (one copy), or semi-limited (two copies).

These terms provide the building blocks for understanding both the mechanics of Yu-Gi-Oh! and the ways these can be influenced by astrological factors. As players deepen their knowledge of these concepts, they can begin to see how the strategic use of cards can mirror the dynamic forces of astrology, enhancing their gameplay and dueling strategy.

Astrological Terminology
Basic Astrological Concepts

- **Zodiac Signs:** The twelve astrological signs each correspond to a 30-degree segment of the 360-degree ecliptic. The signs are Aries, Taurus, Gemini, Cancer, Leo, Virgo, Libra, Scorpio, Sagittarius, Capricorn, Aquarius, and Pisces. Each sign is associated with specific traits and is influenced by one of the four elements (Fire, Earth, Air, Water).

- **Planets:** In astrology, the planets (including the Sun and Moon) are considered as energy mediators that influence life on Earth. Each planet governs different aspects of life and personality:
  - **Sun:** Represents the core essence, ego, and vitality.
  - **Moon:** Governs emotions, instincts, and subconscious needs.
  - **Mercury:** Rules communication, intellect, and information processing.
  - **Venus:** Associated with love, beauty, and values.
  - **Mars:** Represents action, desire, and aggression.
  - **Jupiter:** Signifies growth, expansion, and philosophy.
  - **Saturn:** Associated with structure, discipline, and limitations.
  - **Uranus:** Symbolizes innovation, rebellion, and sudden changes.
  - **Neptune:** Relates to dreams, intuition, and spiritual realms.
  - **Pluto:** Rules transformation, power dynamics, and regeneration.

Technical Astrological Terms

- **Houses:** The twelve sections of a horoscope, each representing different areas of life. The Ascendant (rising sign) marks the beginning of the first house. Houses affect how the energies of the planets and signs are manifested.

- **Aspects**: The angular relationships between two points in a horoscope. They indicate how planets interact and influence each other:
    - **Conjunction** (0 degrees): Intensifies the energies of the combined planets.
    - **Sextile** (60 degrees): Represents opportunities and talents.
    - **Square** (90 degrees): Indicates challenges and conflicts.
    - **Trine** (120 degrees): Signifies harmony and flow.
    - **Opposition** (180 degrees): Points to tension and external struggles.
- **Transits**: The movement of planets across the sky and their current positions relative to one's natal (birth) chart. Transits can activate energies in the natal chart, triggering events and personal developments.
- **Progressions**: An advanced technique that moves the planets in the birth chart forward to reflect personal growth and evolution over time.
- **Retrograde**: Describes a planet's apparent backward motion through the zodiac from Earth's perspective. It symbolizes a time of review and reassessment in the areas governed by the retrograde planet.
- **Eclipses**: Significant astrological events that occur when the Sun, Moon, and Earth align. Solar eclipses (new moons) and lunar eclipses (full moons) can herald major beginnings and endings.
- **Equinoxes and Solstices**: The equinoxes (spring and autumn) and solstices (summer and winter) are points in the year that mark significant shifts and are often used in astrological prognostication.

Advanced Astrological Techniques

- **Synastry**: The comparison of two astrological charts to assess the dynamics of a relationship.
- **Composite Chart**: A chart created from two individual charts, used to represent the relationship itself.
- **Horary Astrology**: An ancient branch of astrology used to answer specific questions by casting a chart for the time the question is posed.
- **Electional Astrology**: The art of choosing the most auspicious time to begin an activity or event based on the astrological conditions.

This glossary of astrological terms equips duelists with the foundational knowledge required to incorporate astrological insights into their Yu-Gi-Oh! strategies. By understanding these concepts, players can begin to harness the cosmic energies that influence the dueling arena, blending celestial wisdom with card game tactics to maximize their gameplay experience.

Appendix B: Astrological Tables and Charts

In "Yugioh Astrology: Astrological Guide to Decks, Duels, and More," astrological tables and charts serve as essential tools to help duelists align their gameplay with celestial influences. This appendix provides comprehensive tables and charts that detail the characteristics of Zodiac signs, the astrological influences on Yu-Gi-Oh! cards and strategies, and a Moon phase calendar to strategically plan duels.

Zodiac Sign Characteristics Table

This table provides a detailed overview of each Zodiac sign, including dates, ruling planets, elements, qualities, and key personality traits which could influence dueling styles.

Zodiac Sign	Date Range	Ruling Planet(s)	Element	Quality	Keywords
Aries	Mar 21 - Apr 19	Mars	Fire	Cardinal	Energetic, assertive, pioneering
Taurus	Apr 20 - May 20	Venus	Earth	Fixed	Reliable, patient, luxurious
Gemini	May 21 - Jun 20	Mercury	Air	Mutable	Curious, adaptable, communicative
Cancer	Jun 21 - Jul 22	Moon	Water	Cardinal	Emotional, nurturing, protective
Leo	Jul 23 - Aug 22	Sun	Fire	Fixed	Dramatic, confident, leader

Virgo	Aug 23 - Sep 22	Mercury	Earth	Mutable	Analytical, practical, diligent
Libra	Sep 23 - Oct 22	Venus	Air	Cardinal	Balanced, fair, aesthetic
Scorpio	Oct 23 - Nov 21	Pluto, Mars	Water	Fixed	Intense, strategic, magnetic
Sagittarius	Nov 22 - Dec 21	Jupiter	Fire	Mutable	Philosophical, adventurous, blunt
Capricorn	Dec 22 - Jan 19	Saturn	Earth	Cardinal	Disciplined, ambitious, cautious
Aquarius	Jan 20 - Feb 18	Uranus, Saturn	Air	Fixed	Innovative, humanitarian, aloof
Pisces	Feb 19 - Mar 20	Neptune, Jupiter	Water	Mutable	Imaginative, empathetic, elusive

Planetary Influences on Cards Chart

This chart aligns the planets with their influences over specific types of Yu-Gi-Oh! cards and strategies, offering guidance on how planetary movements can affect gameplay.

Planet	Card Types Influenced	Strategy Influences

Sun	Hero, Warrior, and Beast-Warrior	Leadership, vitality, power-focused
Moon	Aqua, Fairy	Adaptability, protective strategies
Mercury	Spellcaster, Quick-Play Spell	Communication, fast decisions
Venus	Fairy, Continuous Spell	Harmony, resource attraction
Mars	Warrior, Fire	Aggression, direct attacks
Jupiter	Beast, Expansive Spell	Growth, luck, big plays
Saturn	Rock, Counter Trap	Restriction, enduring strategies
Uranus	Machine, Disruptive Spell/Trap	Innovation, sudden changes
Neptune	Sea Serpent, Illusion Magic	Subterfuge, mystical strategies
Pluto	Fiend, Transformation Magic	Control, elimination, rebirth themes

Moon Phase Calendar for Dueling: 2024-2025

In "Yugioh Astrology: Astrological Guide to Decks, Duels, and More," understanding the phases of the Moon can significantly enhance a duelist's ability to choose the best times for beginning new ventures or maximizing their strategies during competitions. This Moon Phase Calendar provides detailed information about the major phases of the Moon for the years 2024 and 2025, specifically tailored to help duelists plan their activities according to lunar cycles.

2024 Moon Phase Calendar

Date	Moon Phase	Dueling Tips
Jan 24	New Moon	Ideal for testing new decks; fresh starts.
Feb 8	Full Moon	Perfect for high-stakes duels; energy is high.
Feb 22	New Moon	Good for revising strategies; reset and reflect.
Mar 8	Full Moon	Use proven strategies; confidence peaks.
Mar 23	New Moon	Experiment with unconventional tactics.

Apr 6	Full Moon	Leverage strengths; push for victories.
Apr 21	New Moon	Low-key duels; focus on learning, not winning.
May 6	Full Moon	Showcase your best decks; ideal for tournaments.
May 20	New Moon	Reflect on past losses; plan improvements.
Jun 4	Full Moon	Emotional peak; manage stress, stay focused.
Jun 19	New Moon	Test new cards; seek feedback and adjust.
Jul 3	Full Moon	High energy; aggressive strategies favor.
Jul 18	New Moon	Rebuild or overhaul decks; creative thinking.
Aug 2	Full Moon	Capitalize on what works; maintain momentum.
Aug 16	New Moon	Quiet reflection; analyze your game play.
Aug 31	Full Moon	Assert dominance in duels; powerful plays.

Date	Moon Phase	Dueling Tips
Sep 15	New Moon	Set new goals; consider different tactics.
Sep 29	Full Moon	Peak clarity; execute complex strategies.
Oct 14	New Moon	Low energy; focus on defense.
Oct 29	Full Moon	Embrace bold moves; take risks.
Nov 12	New Moon	Plan for future duels; strategic withdrawal.
Nov 28	Full Moon	Optimal for decisive victories; all in.
Dec 12	New Moon	End old rivalries; prepare for new challenges.
Dec 27	Full Moon	Celebratory duels; enjoy the festive season.

2025 Moon Phase Calendar

Date	Moon Phase	Dueling Tips
Jan 11	New Moon	Fresh year; set ambitious goals for dueling.
Jan 26	Full Moon	Harness high energy; focus on winning big duels.

Feb 9	New Moon	Ideal for creative deck building; innovate.
Feb 25	Full Moon	Use tactical advantage; push for leaderboard.
Mar 11	New Moon	Reassess strategies; eliminate weaknesses.
Mar 27	Full Moon	Strong follow-through; capitalize on gains.
Apr 9	New Moon	Focus on forming new alliances; teamwork.
Apr 24	Full Moon	Powerful energy; enforce your will in duels.
May 9	New Moon	Detach from past defeats; clear mindset.
May 24	Full Moon	Emotional intensity; channel emotions strategically.
Jun 7	New Moon	Explore new tactics; diversify your play style.
Jun 22	Full Moon	High success rate; apply pressure on opponents.
Jul 7	New Moon	Withdraw, reflect, prepare for next phase.

Jul 22	Full Moon	Utilize full potential; aim for top performance.
Aug 6	New Moon	Restrategize; integrate new cards.
Aug 21	Full Moon	Display mastery; showcase skills in tournaments.
Sep 5	New Moon	Retreat, analyze recent games; plan upgrades.
Sep 20	Full Moon	Dominance in play; assertive and confident tactics.
Oct 4	New Moon	Renewal phase; rework strategies.
Oct 20	Full Moon	Peak duel performance; utilize strong lunar energy.
Nov 3	New Moon	Reflect on year's progress; focus on personal best.
Nov 18	Full Moon	Close year strongly; use learned experiences.
Dec 3	New Moon	Settle scores; prepare for new beginnings.
Dec 18	Full Moon	Celebrate achievements; end year on high note.

This detailed Moon Phase Calendar provides duelists with specific tips tailored to the energies of each lunar phase, helping to strategically plan duels and tournaments. By aligning their dueling activities with the phases of the Moon, players can maximize their potential for success and personal fulfillment in the game.

Appendix C: Recommended Yu-Gi-Oh! Decks for Each Zodiac Sign

In "Yugioh Astrology: Astrological Guide to Decks, Duels, and More," aligning a duelist's astrological traits with their deck can enhance both gameplay and personal connection to the game. This appendix provides recommended decks for each Zodiac sign, including sample deck configurations and a strategic overview of how these decks capitalize on each sign's unique astrological strengths.

Aries (March 21 - April 19)

Deck: Fire Fist

Strategy: Aries duelists thrive on aggressive tactics and quick wins, making the Fire Fist deck ideal. This deck allows Aries to take charge with powerful monster effects that activate from both the field and the graveyard, pushing for rapid, decisive victories.

Taurus (April 20 - May 20)

Deck: Monarch Control

Strategy: Taurus players value stability and control, traits catered to by the Monarch deck. This deck doesn't rely on the Extra Deck, instead focusing on Tribute Summons for powerful effects that disrupt opponents and provide resource control.

Gemini (May 21 - June 20)

Deck: ABC Dragon Buster

Strategy: Geminis excel with flexible strategies and quick adaptability, which the ABC Dragon Buster deck offers. This deck combines different pieces that can be used together or separately, perfect for Gemini's changing play style and tactical versatility.

Cancer (June 21 - July 22)

Deck: Paleozoic Frogs

Strategy: Cancers are defensive and reactive players. Paleozoic Frogs is a deck that builds a strong defensive line with Trap Cards, then capitalizes on opportunities to summon powerful monsters from seemingly nowhere, mirroring Cancer's protective yet opportunistic nature.

Leo (July 23 - August 22)

Deck: Salamangreat

Strategy: Leos are bold and thrive on being in the spotlight, much like the Salamangreat deck which performs consistently under pressure and can recycle its resources, allowing for flashy, powerful plays and resilience, fitting for a Leo's regal demeanor.

Virgo (August 23 - September 22)

Deck: Trickstar

Strategy: Virgos are meticulous and enjoy detailed, complex strategies. Trickstars can inflict damage with precise, incremental effects, a playstyle that rewards attention to detail and strategic planning typical of Virgos.

Libra (September 23 - October 22)

Deck: Sky Striker

Strategy: Libras seek balance and fairness, qualities reflected in the Sky Striker deck's ability to adapt and control the pace of the game. This deck's strategic depth and its ability to respond to various threats align well with Libra's desire for equilibrium.

Scorpio (October 23 - November 21)

Deck: Dark World

Strategy: Scorpios are intense and strategic, traits that sync well with the Dark World deck, which revolves around discarding as a cost to trigger powerful and often disruptive effects, aligning with Scorpio's love for transformation and control.

Sagittarius (November 22 - December 21)

Deck: Lightsworn

Strategy: Sagittarians are adventurous and optimistic, making the high-risk, high-reward style of the Lightsworn deck a perfect match. This deck mills cards for powerful effects, which can lead to dramatic comebacks, mirroring Sagittarius's love for a dynamic challenge.

Capricorn (December 22 - January 19)

Deck: True Draco

Strategy: Capricorns are disciplined and manage resources carefully, which makes the True Draco deck ideal. It focuses on Tribute Summons and continuous spells/traps to control the field and resources, perfectly aligning with Capricorn's strategic and managerial skills.

Aquarius (January 20 - February 18)

Deck: Cyber Dragon

Strategy: Aquarians are innovative and group-oriented. The Cyber Dragon deck, with its ability to fuse machines for various effects and summon powerful monsters quickly, suits Aquarius's futuristic and collective approach.

Pisces (February 19 - March 20)

Deck: Mermail Atlantean

Strategy: Pisces are intuitive and adaptable, traits well-suited to the Mermail Atlantean deck, which is fluid and powerful, focusing on creating chains of monster effects that adapt to the current game state, reflecting Pisces's mutable nature.

These decks are designed to resonate with the astrological characteristics of each sign, enhancing the dueling experience by aligning strategic preferences with celestial influences. By choosing a deck that reflects their Zodiac traits, duelists can engage more deeply with Yu-Gi-Oh!, maximizing both their enjoyment and effectiveness in the game.

Appendix D: Astrological Software and Tools

In "Yugioh Astrology: Astrological Guide to Decks, Duels, and More," the integration of astrology into Yu-Gi-Oh! strategies is significantly enhanced by the use of specialized software and online tools. This appendix provides a curated list of recommended astrological software for calculating and interpreting astrological charts, as well as a selection of online resources for Yu-Gi-Oh! deck building and testing.

Astrological Software Recommendations

Astrological software can range from basic chart calculators to complex programs that offer in-depth interpretations and advanced prognostic features. Here are several highly recommended options for both beginners and advanced users:

1. **Solar Fire**: This is a premium astrology software widely used by professional astrologers. It offers robust features for casting and comparing charts, calculating precise astrological transits, progressions, and returns, and even electional astrology functionalities.

2. **AstroSeek**: Offering both free and paid services, AstroSeek provides users with reliable chart calculations, transit forecasts, and personalized astrological reports. It is particularly user-friendly for beginners.

3. **TimePassages**: Ideal for both novices and professionals, TimePassages offers accurate astrological readings, easy-to-understand interpretations, and tools for generating and analyzing natal and transit charts.

4. **Astro.com**: Known for its high accuracy and depth, Astro.com allows users to create an astrological chart for free and provides a range of free reports, with more detailed analyses available for purchase.

5. **Janus**: Janus is noted for its comprehensive range of features including natal, transit, progression, and synastry interpretations, making it suitable for both educational purposes and professional depth analysis.

Yu-Gi-Oh! Deck-Building Tools

Building and testing Yu-Gi-Oh! decks require careful strategy and planning. Several online tools have been developed to assist duelists in this process, from deck construction to simulation against other players. Here are some valuable resources:

1. **YGOPro**: A fully automated simulator, YGOPro allows players to test their decks against others in real-time. It updates with new cards and rules, ensuring players have access to the latest data.
2. **Dueling Nexus**: An online, automated trading card game platform that plays similarly to YGOPro but operates directly through a web browser. It is easy to access and requires no download.
3. **Duelingbook**: A manual simulator, Duelingbook offers players a platform that mimics the real-life playing experience as closely as possible. Players make all moves manually, offering a high level of control.
4. **DeckBox**: While not specifically for Yu-Gi-Oh!, DeckBox provides excellent tools for managing card inventories and building decks. It can be useful for theorycrafting and organizational purposes.
5. **Yugioh Top Decks**: This website is particularly useful for keeping track of popular and successful deck configurations used in tournaments. It is a great resource for seeing how top players construct their decks, providing insights into effective deck building strategies.

These software and tools are indispensable for duelists looking to integrate astrological insights into their Yu-Gi-Oh! gameplay. Whether calculating the perfect moment for a duel using astrological software or building a deck tailored to astrological strengths, these resources provide duelists with the necessary tools to enhance their strategic edge.

Appendix E: List of Useful Astrological and Yu-Gi-Oh! Resources

"Yugioh Astrology: Astrological Guide to Decks, Duels, and More" integrates two rich subjects, each with its own dedicated following and extensive resources. This appendix aims to provide duelists and astrologers with a comprehensive resource list, including essential readings and active online communities to deepen understanding and enhance practical skills.

Books and Guides

Yu-Gi-Oh!:

1. **"Yu-Gi-Oh! Official Handbook" by Tracey West** - An excellent starting point for beginners, providing an overview of the game's rules, card types, and basic strategies.
2. **"Yu-Gi-Oh! Duelist's Resource: Strategies and Tips" by Eliot Carter** - A deeper dive into advanced tactics, deck building, and competitive play.
3. **"Mastering Duel Monsters" by Brian Reese** - Focuses on high-level competitive play and strategies used in major tournaments.

Astrology:

1. **"The Only Astrology Book You'll Ever Need" by Joanna Martine Woolfolk** - A comprehensive guide that covers everything from understanding your sun sign to predicting your future.
2. **"Parker's Astrology: The Definitive Guide to Using Astrology in Every Aspect of Your Life" by Julia and Derek Parker** - Offers detailed explanations of astrological concepts, including

relationships, career, and health, with rich illustrations and diagrams.

3. **"Astrology for the Soul" by Jan Spiller** - Explores the North Node and its significance in personal growth and life direction, offering a spiritual approach to astrology.

Online Communities and Forums

Yu-Gi-Oh!:

1. **Duelingbook** - An online Yu-Gi-Oh! platform that allows for manual play. Its forums are active with discussions on deck building, strategies, and game rules (duelingbook.com).
2. **Reddit r/yugioh** - A vibrant subreddit where enthusiasts discuss the latest cards, news, and strategies. Users share deck builds and participate in discussions about the competitive scene.
3. **Pojo.com** - One of the oldest Yu-Gi-Oh! communities with extensive forums discussing various aspects of the game, including card rulings, strategies, and tournament play.

Astrology:

1. **Astro.com Forum** - A highly respected forum where both amateurs and professionals discuss a variety of astrological topics. Great for getting charts interpreted or learning new techniques.
2. **Reddit r/astrology** - A subreddit dedicated to astrology where users share experiences, ask questions about their birth charts, and discuss current astrological events.
3. **The Astrology Podcast** - Provides discussions, interviews, and educational content on traditional and modern astrological practices. Available on various platforms including Spotify and Apple Podcasts.

Coordinated Dueling Platforms

1. **YGOPro** - An automated system for playing Yu-Gi-Oh! online with people from around the world. It includes all the latest cards and is constantly updated.
2. **Dueling Nexus** - Similar to YGOPro, Dueling Nexus runs directly in a web browser and provides a user-friendly interface for new players.

These resources are tailored to foster a deep and ongoing engagement with both Yu-Gi-Oh! and astrology. Whether you are looking to master the game, understand the celestial influences on your life and dueling strategies, or connect with like-minded enthusiasts, this curated list provides valuable starting points for exploration and community engagement.

Appendix F: Full Moon and New Moon Dates
In "Yugioh Astrology: Astrological Guide to Decks, Duels, and More," timing your duels or deck-building sessions according to the lunar cycle can potentially enhance your strategic effectiveness, as many astrologers believe that lunar phases affect human behavior and energy levels. This appendix provides a comprehensive list of Full Moon and New Moon dates over the next five years, alongside explanations of their astrological significance.

Astrological Significance of Lunar Phases

- **New Moon**: The New Moon marks the beginning of the lunar cycle and is a time for setting intentions, starting new projects, or initiating change. In Yu-Gi-Oh!, this is an auspicious time to test new decks or strategies, as the energies associated with new beginnings can lend momentum to your efforts.
- **Full Moon**: Occurring roughly two weeks after the New Moon, the Full Moon represents a time of fulfillment and culmination. Energy and emotions can run high during this phase, making it ideal for competitive dueling where high energy can be advantageous. The Full Moon is also a perfect time for analyzing the progress of your strategies, as the increased light can symbolize greater clarity and insight.

Full Moon and New Moon Dates
2024

Date	Phase
January 25	New Moon
February 24	Full Moon

March 25	New Moon
April 23	Full Moon
May 24	New Moon
June 22	Full Moon
July 23	New Moon
August 21	Full Moon
September 19	New Moon
October 19	Full Moon
November 17	New Moon
December 17	Full Moon

2025

Date	Phase
January 16	New Moon
February 15	Full Moon
March 17	New Moon
April 15	Full Moon
May 16	New Moon
June 14	Full Moon
July 16	New Moon
August 13	Full Moon
September 11	New Moon

October 11	Full Moon
November 10	New Moon
December 10	Full Moon

2026

Date	Phase
January 9	New Moon
February 8	Full Moon
March 10	New Moon
April 8	Full Moon
May 9	New Moon
June 7	Full Moon
July 8	New Moon
August 6	Full Moon
September 5	New Moon
October 4	Full Moon
November 4	New Moon
December 4	Full Moon

2027

Date	Phase

January 3	New Moon
February 2	Full Moon
March 4	New Moon
April 3	Full Moon
May 3	New Moon
June 2	Full Moon
July 2	New Moon
August 1	Full Moon
August 31	New Moon
September 29	Full Moon
October 30	New Moon
November 29	Full Moon

2028

Date	Phase
January 28	New Moon
February 27	Full Moon
March 28	New Moon
April 26	Full Moon
May 27	New Moon
June 25	Full Moon
July 25	New Moon

August 24	Full Moon
September 23	New Moon
October 22	Full Moon
November 21	New Moon
December 21	Full Moon

This comprehensive schedule of lunar phases will help duelists plan their major events and duels, aligning their activities with the natural rhythms of the moon to maximize effectiveness and harness the energies believed to be available during these significant astrological moments.

<u>Message from the Author:</u>

I hope you enjoyed this book, I love astrology and knew there was not a book such as this out on the shelf. I love metaphysical items as well. Please check out my other books:

-Life of Government Benefits

-My life of Hell

-My life with Hydrocephalus

-Red Sky

-World Domination:Woman's rule

-World Domination:Woman's Rule 2: The War

-Life and Banishment of Apophis: book 1

-The Kidney Friendly Diet

-The Ultimate Hemp Cookbook

-Creating a Dispensary(legally)

-Cleanliness throughout life: the importance of showering from childhood to adulthood.

-Strong Roots: The Risks of Overcoddling children

-Hemp Horoscopes: Cosmic Insights and Earthly Healing

- Celestial Hemp Navigating the Zodiac: Through the Green Cosmos

-Astrological Hemp: Aligning The Stars with Earth's Ancient Herb

-The Astrological Guide to Hemp: Stars, Signs, and Sacred Leaves

-Green Growth: Innovative Marketing Strategies for your Hemp Products and Dispensary

-Cosmic Cannabis

-Astrological Munchies

-Henry The Hemp

-Zodiacal Roots: The Astrological Soul Of Hemp

- Green Constellations: Intersection of Hemp and Zodiac

-Hemp in The Houses: An astrological Adventure Through The Cannabis Galaxy

-Galactic Ganja Guide

Heavenly Hemp

Zodiac Leaves

Doctor Who Astrology

Cannastrology

Stellar Satvias and Cosmic Indicas

Celestial Cannabis: A Zodiac Journey

AstroHerbology: The Sky and The Soil: Volume 1

AstroHerbology:Celestial Cannabis:Volume 2

Cosmic Cannabis Cultivation

The Starry Guide to Herbal Harmony: Volume 1

The Starry Guide to Herbal Harmony: Cannabis Universe: Volume 2

Check out my Virtual dispensary for all your hemp needs: https://shift.store/sg1fan23477/retail

If you want solar for your home go here: https://www.harborsolar.live/apophisenterprises/

Instagrams: @apophis_enterprises, @hempkingdom2024,
@apophisbookemporium,
@apophisfashion,
@apophisscardshop
Twitter: @apophisenterpr1, Tiktok:@apophisenterprise
Youtube: @sg1fan23477
Podcast: Apophis Chat Zone: https://open.spotify.com/show/5zXbrCLEV2xzCp8ybrfHsk?si=fb4d4fdbdce44dec
Newsletter: https://apophiss-newsletter-27c897.beehiiv.com/

Journal: